Hide and

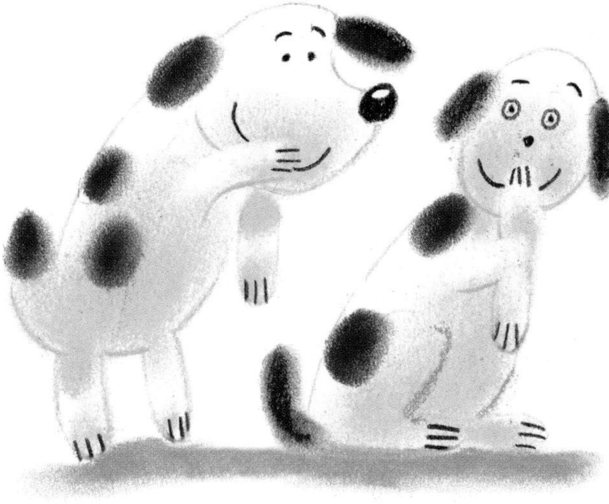

by Barbara Wood
illustrated by Robert Hefferan

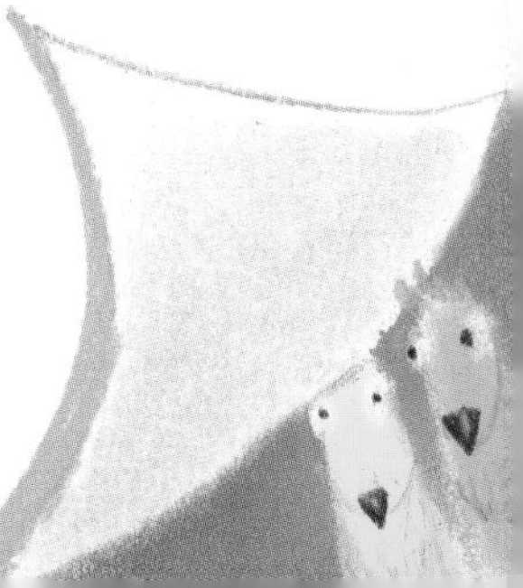

HAMPTON-BROWN

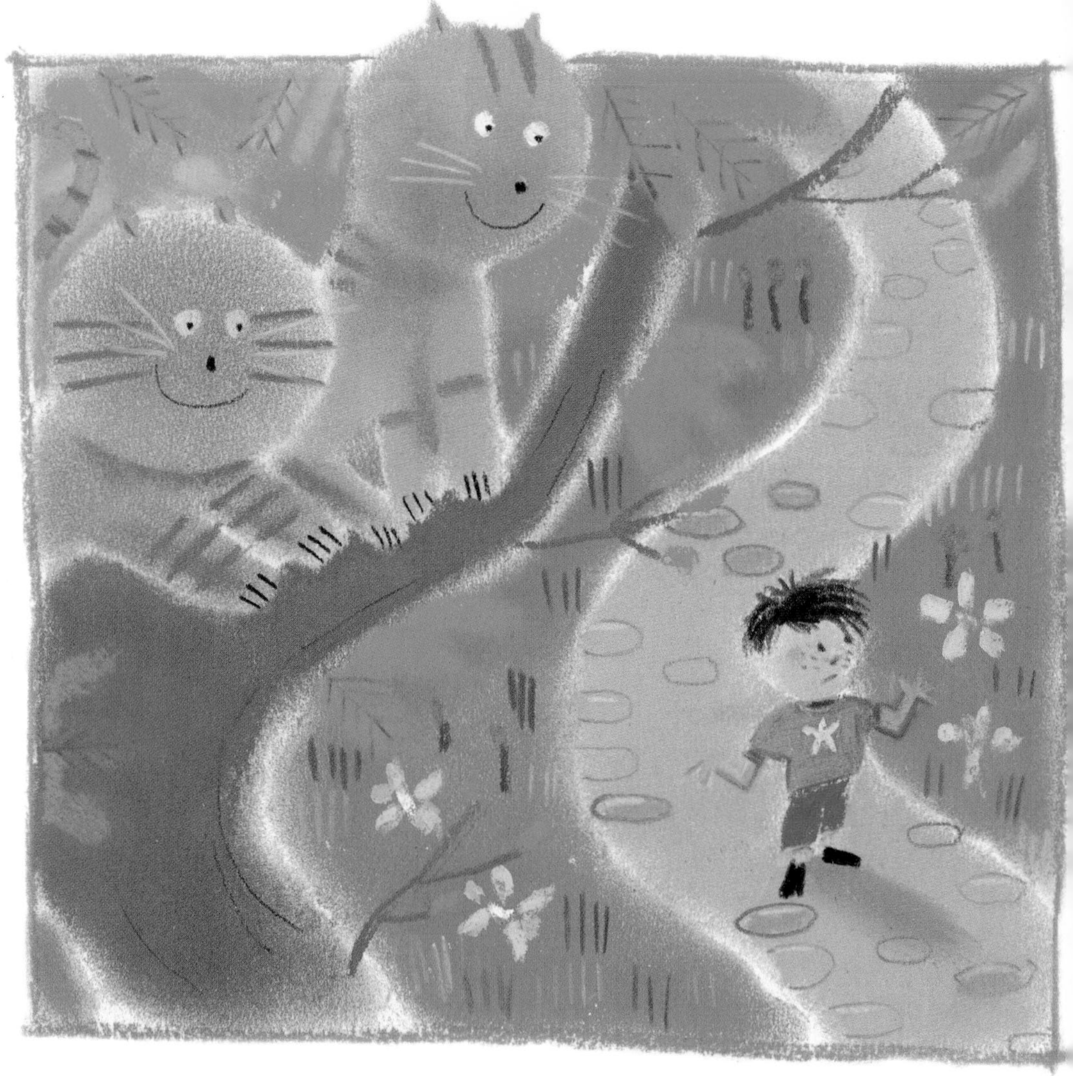

Where are the cats?

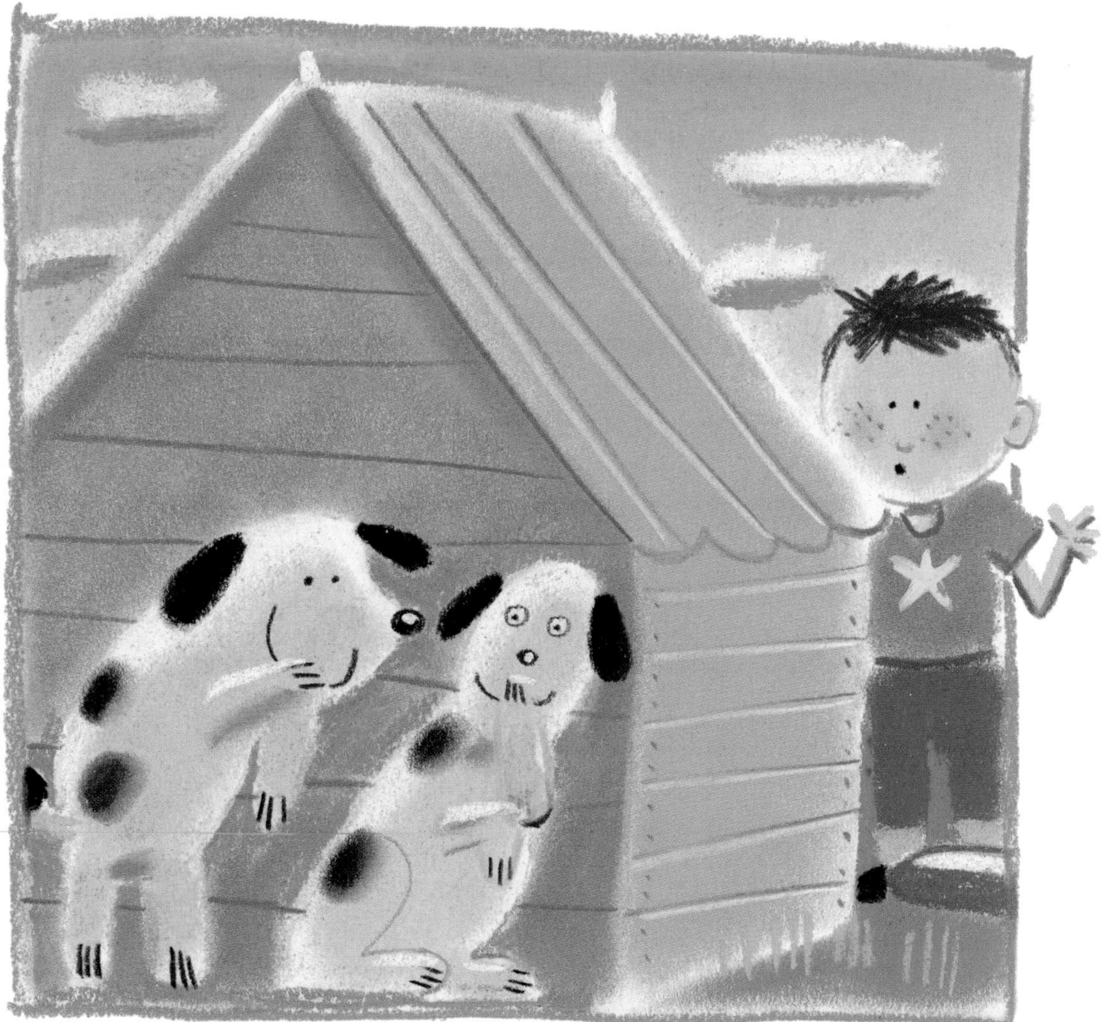

Where are the dogs?

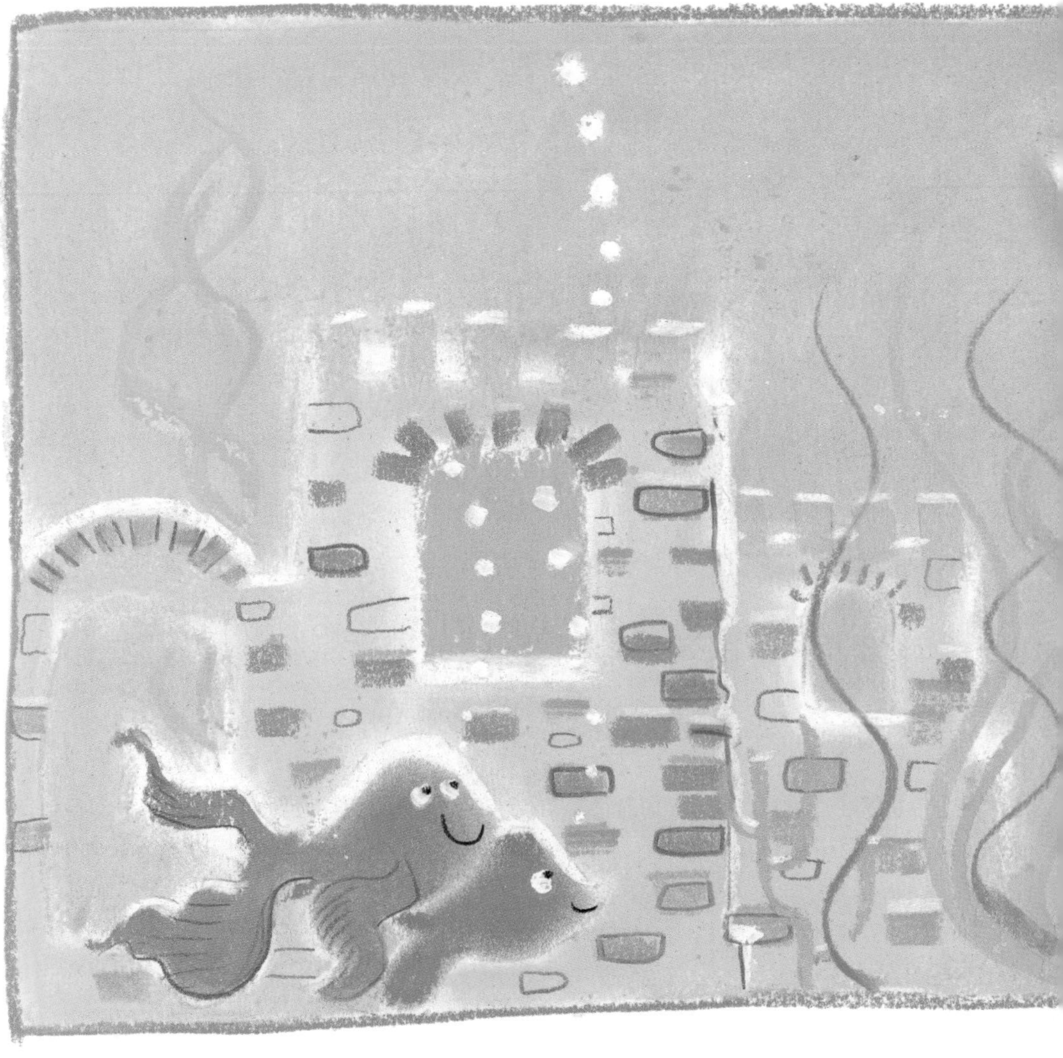

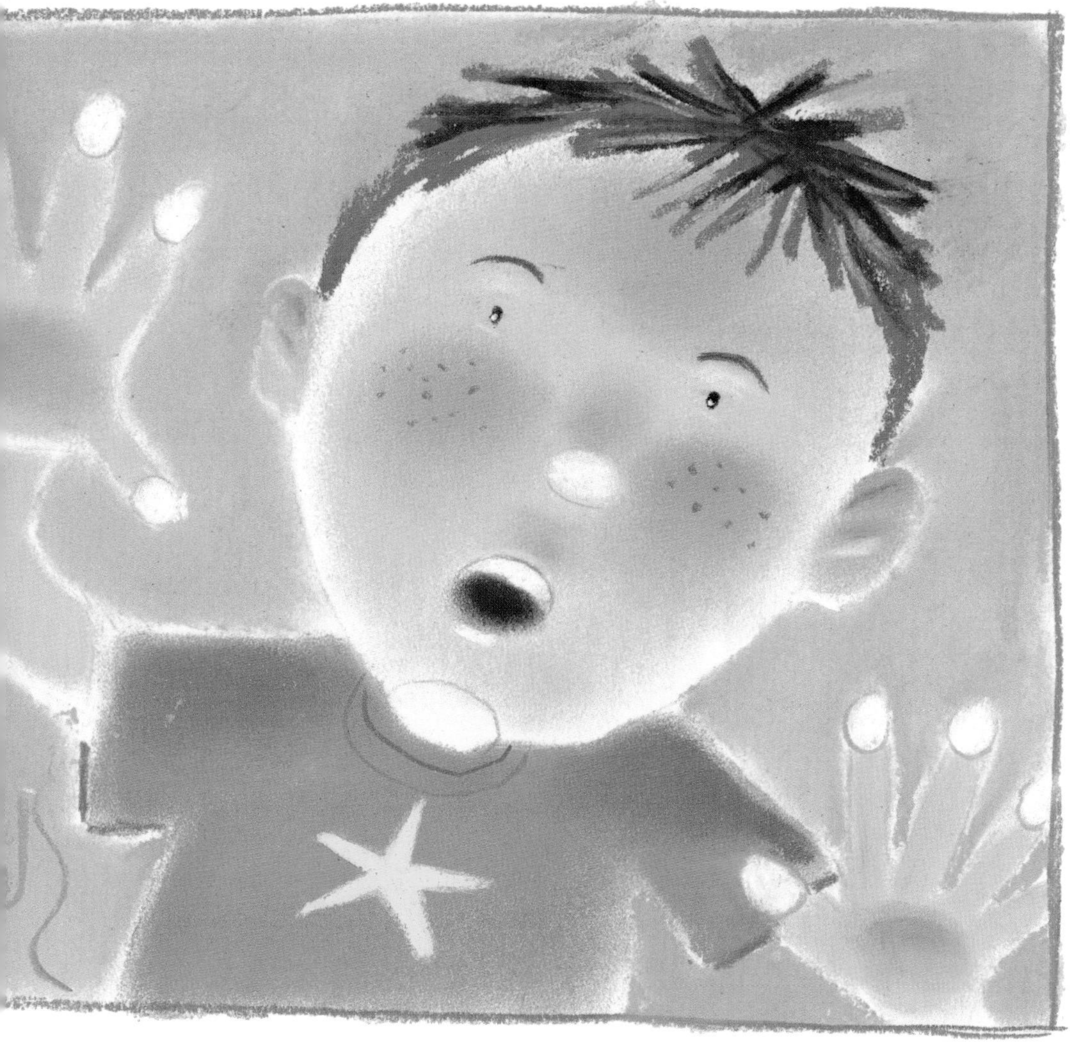

Where are the fish?

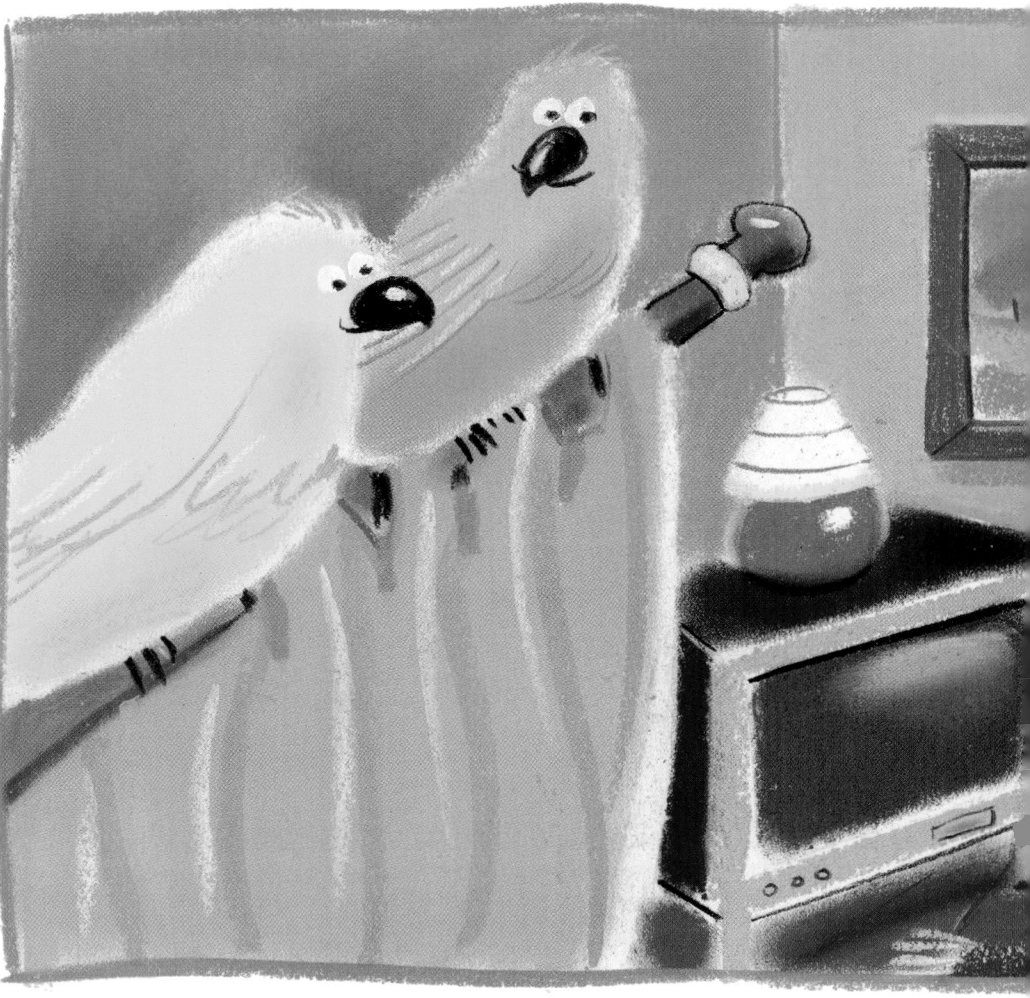

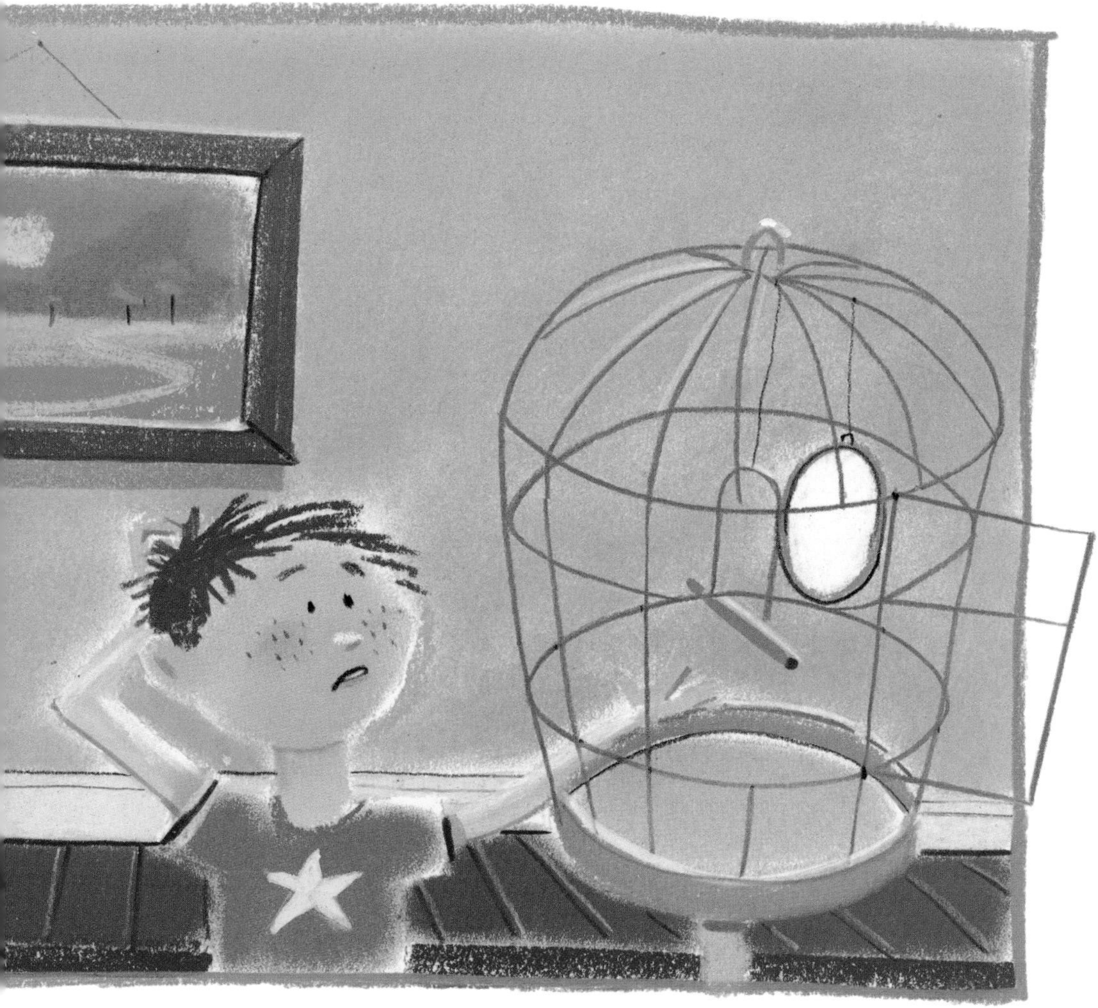

Where are the birds?

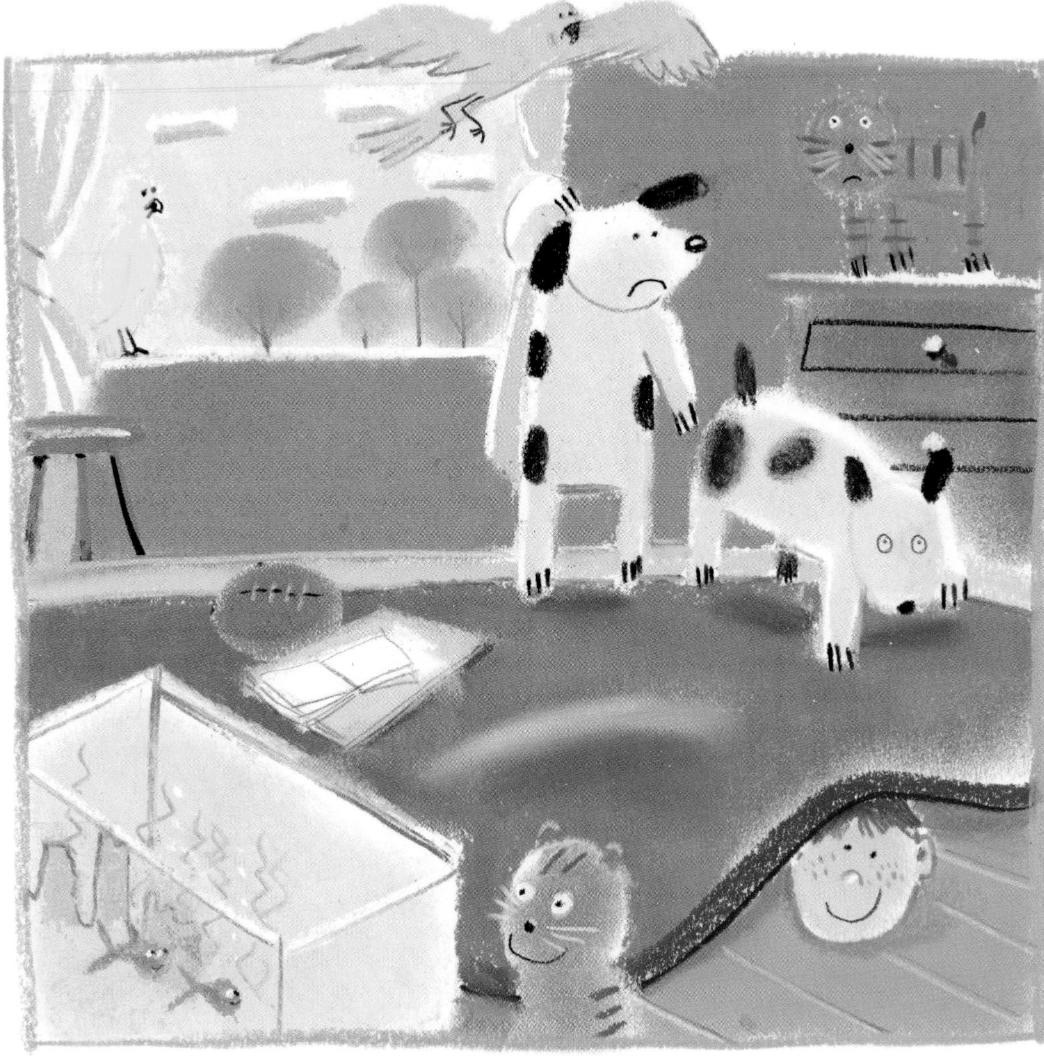

Where is Sam?